Girls' Health™

The Female Reproductive System

Sophie Waters

rosen publishing's
rosen central®

New York

Published in 2008 by The Rosen Publishing Group, Inc.
29 East 21st Street, New York, NY 10010

Library of Congress Cataloging-in-Publication Data

Waters, Sophie.
The female reproductive system / Sophie Waters.
     p. cm.—(Girls' health)
Includes bibliographical references.
ISBN-13: 978-1-4042-1950-2
ISBN-10: 1-4042-1950-1
1. Generative organs, Female—Juvenile literature. 2. Human reproduction—Juvenile literature. 3. Pregnancy—Juvenile literature. 4. Birth control—Juvenile literature.
I. Title.
QP259.W38 2007
612.6'2—dc22

                                                        2006101218

Manufactured in the United States of America

Contents

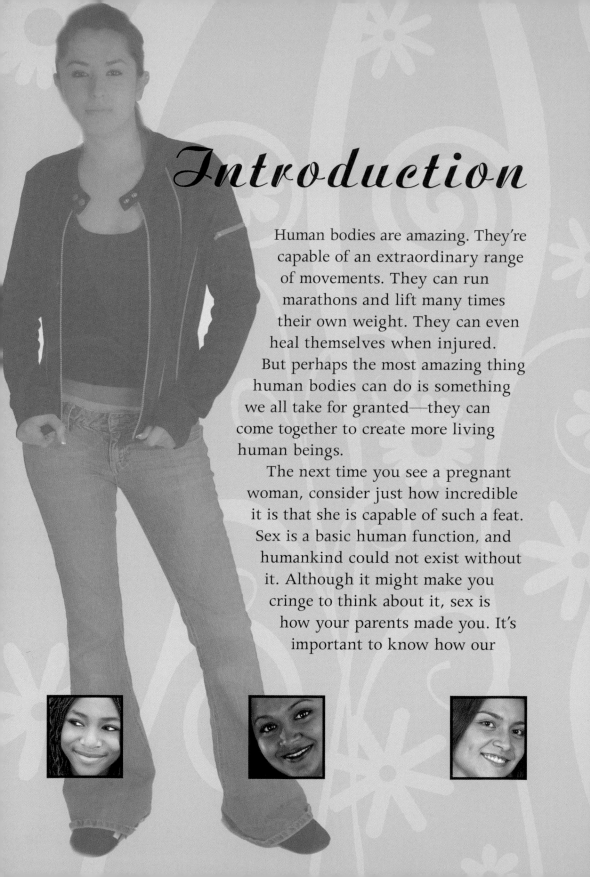

Introduction

Human bodies are amazing. They're capable of an extraordinary range of movements. They can run marathons and lift many times their own weight. They can even heal themselves when injured.

But perhaps the most amazing thing human bodies can do is something we all take for granted—they can come together to create more living human beings.

The next time you see a pregnant woman, consider just how incredible it is that she is capable of such a feat. Sex is a basic human function, and humankind could not exist without it. Although it might make you cringe to think about it, sex is how your parents made you. It's important to know how our

bodies reproduce. The first step is to understand your own body, inside and out.

This book explains the process of reproduction from a girl's perspective. You'll get a clear idea of what your role is in reproduction, and you'll see which body parts and systems are involved. You'll also see what happens to a girl's body when she's pregnant. There's a discussion of the benefits of virginity and abstinence (choosing not to have sex). Finally, you'll read about the hugely important choices you will have to make if and when you decide to become sexually active.

Reproduction and your sexuality are complicated issues, but they are not impossible to figure out. When you understand the female reproductive system, you can make smarter, more informed decisions. This knowledge will help you grasp the mental, physical, and emotional consequences of your reproductive choices.

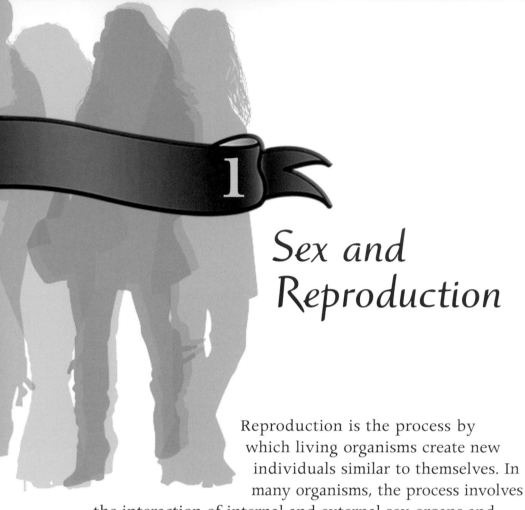

Sex and Reproduction

Reproduction is the process by which living organisms create new individuals similar to themselves. In many organisms, the process involves the interaction of internal and external sex organs and hormones (chemicals that regulate the functioning of organs). Humans, other animals, plants, and even bacteria reproduce.

Maturing for Reproduction

Puberty is the period in your life when you become capable of sexual reproduction. Typically, girls start puberty between ages nine and fourteen, the average age being from ten to twelve years old. Boys go through puberty a bit later. Of course, the age when puberty begins varies from person to person, so you shouldn't worry about your own body's schedule.

All kinds of changes take place before the onset of puberty. These changes signal the passage from childhood to adulthood, marking the beginning of a very exciting—and often confusing—time in a person's life.

Puberty can be bewildering or strange. For one thing, it may seem like your body changes overnight. Your whole body grows. Pimples may appear. Hair starts sprouting up under your arms and around your genitals. You will start thinking differently about your body, boys, and sex. You will begin to menstruate (get your period) and develop breasts. These changes are brought on by hormones.

Hormones and Brain Chemistry

Hormones are chemicals that control how different parts of the body operate. The body makes more than forty kinds of hormones, each with a specific message for a specific organ. The organs of the female reproductive system are controlled by hormones that begin their journey in your brain.

At the center of your brain are the hypothalamus and the pituitary gland. The hypothalamus is a structure that acts like the command center for your entire body. The pituitary is the master gland. Together, they regulate growth, hunger, sleep, and many other activities, including reproduction. When a girl enters puberty, her role in sexual reproduction begins when the hypothalamus sends a hormone to the pituitary gland. Then the pituitary gland sends hormones to the ovaries, small organs located in your abdomen. Inside the ovaries, each of the thousands of female sex cells called ova (eggs) sits inside a sac called a follicle.

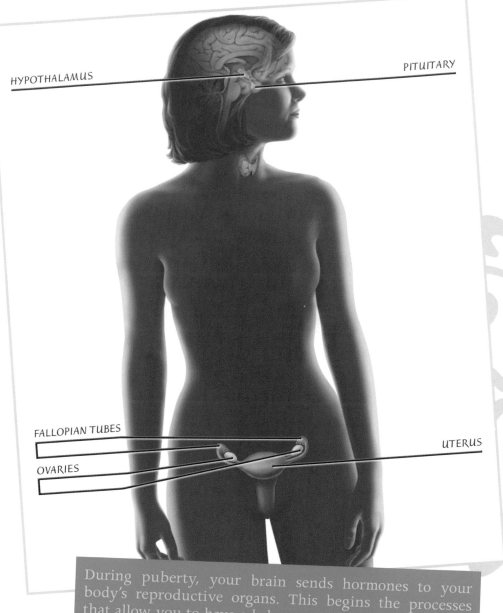

HYPOTHALAMUS

PITUITARY

FALLOPIAN TUBES

OVARIES

UTERUS

During puberty, your brain sends hormones to your body's reproductive organs. This begins the processes that allow you to have a baby.

When the ovaries get the message from the pituitary, they instruct several eggs to start developing.

Ovulation

As the eggs mature, the ovaries release the hormone estrogen. This hormone makes the lining of the uterus thicken. (The uterus is the part of your body in which babies develop.) When the uterus is ready for an egg, the hypothalamus sends another hormone to the pituitary gland, which starts the process of getting an egg to the uterus. The pituitary gland then sends to the ovaries a new type of hormone that makes the most mature follicle burst open and release its egg. This is ovulation. The egg leaves the ovary and finds its way into a fallopian tube (you have one for each ovary). The egg then travels through the fallopian tube to the waiting uterus.

At that time, the broken follicle begins to produce more estrogen and another important hormone called progesterone. These often are called the female hormones. An egg cannot grow properly without a good supply of these two hormones. The follicle produces them the whole time the egg is in the uterus.

Menstruation

If the egg in the uterus is not fertilized, it dies. The follicle will then stop making hormones. Without the hormones, the blood supply to the extra layers of the uterine lining dries up, and the layers start to fall off. The uterine lining is then discharged through the vagina, a time of the month commonly referred to as your period.

Some young female athletes have very little body fat. Maintaining too little body fat can cause you to stop ovulating.

The technical term for your period is menstruation, or menses. Menstruation typically occurs once a month, and it usually lasts from three to seven days. The entire menstrual cycle can take anywhere from twenty-one to thirty-five days, but on average it takes twenty-eight days.

Some girls may stop getting their period even though they aren't pregnant. This is called amenorrhea. It often results when a girl has too little body fat, as is the case with those suffering from the eating disorder anorexia (self-starving). It is also common among girls who train hard for physically demanding sports like gymnastics. Menstruation ends for good when a woman reaches menopause. This usually occurs around age fifty.

Premenstrual Syndrome

Premenstrual syndrome (PMS) is the name for a group of physical and emotional changes that some women go through before their menstrual period begins. The symptoms follow a pattern: they reappear around the same time each month and go away after your period has begun.

Physical changes caused by PMS include breast tenderness or swelling, bloating, weight gain, headache, fatigue, constipation, and increased or decreased appetite. Mental and emotional changes include depression, irritability, anxiety, tension, mood swings, inability to concentrate, and fluctuations (changes) in sex drive. You don't need to have all of these to have PMS, and the severity of symptoms can vary from month to month.

There is no cure for PMS, but there are ways to cope with the symptoms. To prevent swelling, bloating, or breast tenderness, steer clear of salt and caffeine for a couple of weeks before your period. Reducing caffeine (found in coffee, tea, colas, and chocolate) can calm anxiety, insomnia, and irritability, too. If you feel depressed, talk to a close

The uncomfortable symptoms of premenstrual syndrome (PMS) can leave you feeling in a foul mood.

friend, family member, or counselor. Schedule time for energizing exercise, and get extra sleep.

Dysmenorrhea

PMS is not the same as dysmenorrhea, which is the term for the painful spasms that may accompany a woman's menstruation. Usually, the main symptom of dysmenorrhea is cramping in the pelvic area (lower abdomen). The cramping starts about the same time as your period and continues for a few days. Along with cramping, you may have nausea (being sick to your stomach), vomiting, lower back pain, dizziness, tiredness, or bloating.

In the teenage years, dysmenorrhea is more common than PMS. One theory is that the uterine muscles tighten to push out the menstrual blood, and this tightening may cause discomfort. Also, the uterus makes some chemicals of its own, called prostaglandins. Some researchers think girls have menstrual cramps because their prostaglandins are out of balance.

Pregnancy Basics

Human beings, like most animals, reproduce sexually. A human baby is created when a female sex cell and a male sex cell unite. These sex cells are called gametes. Male gametes are called sperm; female gametes are called ova (eggs). When a sperm and an egg unite, fertilization occurs. A fertilized egg may travel to the uterus and implant itself in the uterine lining. This is the beginning of pregnancy, a process that generally lasts about nine months.

When fertilization first takes place, the fertilized egg is smaller than the head of a pin. The fertilized egg grows into a group of

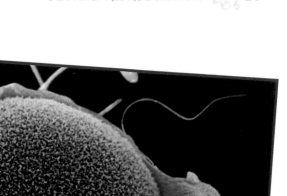
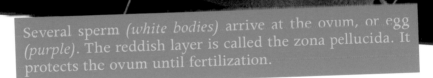

Several sperm *(white bodies)* arrive at the ovum, or egg *(purple)*. The reddish layer is called the zona pellucida. It protects the ovum until fertilization.

cells called an embryo. The embryo then forms tissues that develop into organs. At this point, the embryo is called a fetus. During the rest of the pregnancy, the fetus continues to grow and develop. After about nine months, the fetus is fully developed and can live outside of the mother's body. Pregnancy ends when the woman gives birth to the baby.

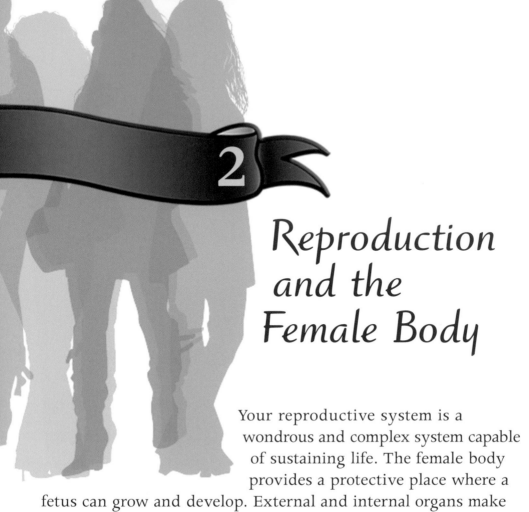

Reproduction and the Female Body

Your reproductive system is a wondrous and complex system capable of sustaining life. The female body provides a protective place where a fetus can grow and develop. External and internal organs make up the female reproductive system.

External Reproductive Organs

The external sex organs are called the genitals. A female's genitals are known as the vulva, which includes parts called the mons veneris, the labia majora, the labia minora, the vestibule, and the clitoris.

The mons veneris is the pad of fatty tissue over the pubic bone. After puberty, it is covered by pubic hair. The labia majora, or outer lips, are the two folds of skin that make up the mons veneris. The labia minora, or inner lips, are the hairless folds of tissue

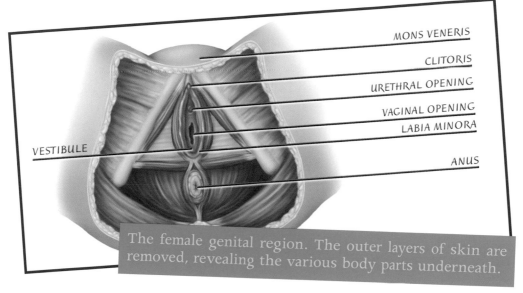

MONS VENERIS

CLITORIS

URETHRAL OPENING

VAGINAL OPENING

LABIA MINORA

VESTIBULE

ANUS

The female genital region. The outer layers of skin are removed, revealing the various body parts underneath.

tucked between the outer lips. These inner lips can be seen by separating the outer lips.

The vestibule is found between the inner lips. The opening of the urethra and the vaginal opening are located in the vestibule, as are two sets of glands. The urethra is a tube that leads from the bladder to the urethral opening. This opening is where urine leaves the body. The vaginal opening is located just behind the urethral opening and is the gateway to your internal reproductive organs. Women have three openings: the anus; the urethral opening; and the vagina, which is where menstrual blood is released. The vaginal opening can be partially covered by a very thin layer of skin called the hymen. Outside the vaginal opening are two sets of small, round Bartholin's glands. When a woman is sexually excited, these glands release fluid.

The clitoris is located where the labia minora join, just above the vestibule. It is a small organ that contains many nerve endings and is very sensitive to touch. The primary function of the clitoris is for producing pleasure.

Internal Reproductive Organs

The reproductive organs found inside your body consist of the vagina, the uterus (which includes the cervix), the fallopian tubes, and the ovaries. Each plays a different part in reproduction.

The Vagina

The vagina is a muscular, tube-shaped organ that leads to the inside of your body. It is about 3 to 5 inches (8 to 13 centimeters) long. Since it is a muscle, its shape and size can expand to fit a male's penis during sexual intercourse, or serve as the birth passage for a baby. During your period, your menstrual blood exits your body through the vagina.

The Uterus

The uterus, or womb, is a thick, hollow organ shaped like an upside-down pear. It is approximately the size of your fist, about 3 inches (8 cm) long and 2 inches (5 cm) wide. It is made of strong muscle that can expand and stretch to hold a baby. In fact, the uterus can expand up to 200 times its normal size during pregnancy! Its job is to receive a fertilized egg and then nourish and protect the embryo until childbirth. Each month, the lining of the uterus builds up in case it needs to provide nourishment for a fertilized egg. If there is no fertilized egg, this lining is shed during menstruation.

The Cervix

The lower third of the uterus is called the cervix. It is narrow and tube-shaped, and is only about 1 inch (3 cm) in diameter.

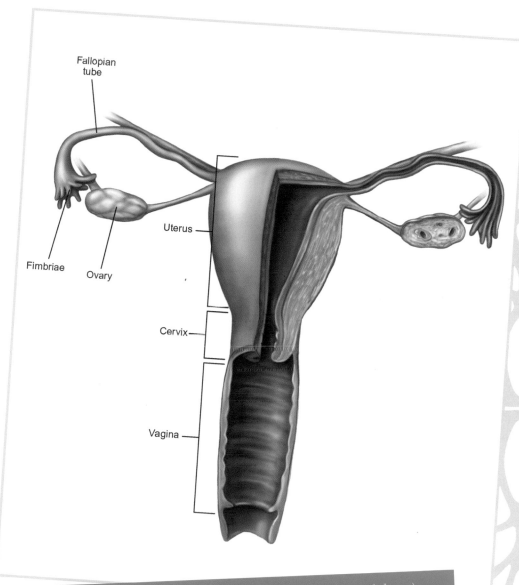

Fallopian
tube

Fimbriae

Ovary

Uterus

Cervix

Vagina

The internal female reproductive organs *(above)* are located in the lower portion of the abdomen, between the bladder and the rectum.

The cervix is located at the upper end of the vagina and serves as a passageway into and out of the uterus. When a woman gives birth, the cervix softens and expands for the baby to come out.

The Fallopian Tubes

Each of your two fallopian tubes are about 4 inches (10 cm) long and extend from both sides of your uterus. The ends of the fallopian tubes are funnel-shaped and lined with fimbriae—moving, finger-like projections that draw an egg into the tube from the ovary.

The Ovaries

The ovaries are about the size and shape of unshelled almonds and are found near the ends of the fallopian tubes on both sides of the uterus. Ovaries contain a female's ova (eggs). In addition, they produce the female hormones estrogen and progesterone.

Secondary Reproductive Organs: The Breasts

The breasts, or mammary glands, are not directly involved with reproduction. However, they play a vital role in the development of the baby. Breasts are sometimes referred to as secondary, or accessory, reproductive organs. The development of a girl's breasts during puberty is triggered by sex hormones, mainly estrogen.

The most obvious external features of developed breasts are the areoles and nipples. The areoles are round, typically pigmented (different-colored) areas located near the center of the breast. They contain glands that keep the breast tips moisturized. Each areola comes to a point at the nipple, a projection that becomes erect when stimulated. The baby sucks on the nipple in order to extract the mother's milk.

10 *Great Questions to Ask Your Doctor*

1. Is it normal to experience huge emotional swings during puberty?

2. Are there things I can do that can make puberty easier?

3. How long does puberty last? What are some changes I should expect?

4. What over-the-counter medication, if any, would you recommend for cramps?

5. What can I do to alleviate symptoms of PMS?

6. When should I see a gynecologist?

7. Besides seeing a doctor, are there things I can do to keep my reproductive system healthy?

8. If I'm interested in birth control, can you help me figure out the best option?

9. Will my parents find out if I start taking birth control pills?

10. How can I protect myself from sexually transmitted diseases? Pregnancy? Is there a way for me to protect against both at the same time?

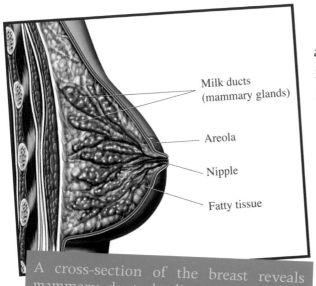

Milk ducts
(mammary glands)

Areola

Nipple

Fatty tissue

A cross-section of the breast reveals mammary ducts leading to the nipple. Chest muscles *(red layers)* lie between the breast and the ribs *(white ovals, left)*.

Behind the areole and nipple, each breast normally contains from five to twenty rounded lobes. These are further divided into smaller lobules that contain cells called alveoli, which are capable of converting the mother's blood into milk. The milk passes through fine ducts, or tubes, that join to form a single larger duct called the lactiferous ("milk producing") duct. The production of milk in the breast is called lactation.

So, each breast has about five to twenty lactiferous ducts that channel the milk toward the nipple. Behind each nipple, the duct opens up to form the ampulla, where the milk is collected and stored for breastfeeding. As the baby suckles, the nipple remains erect, making it easier for the baby to extract the milk from the tip of the nipple.

Lobules inside the breast are surrounded by fat tissue. Breast size is largely determined by the amount of this fat. The breast's ability to supply milk depends on its lobules and not on the fat, so the size of the breast has no relation to the amount of milk it can produce.

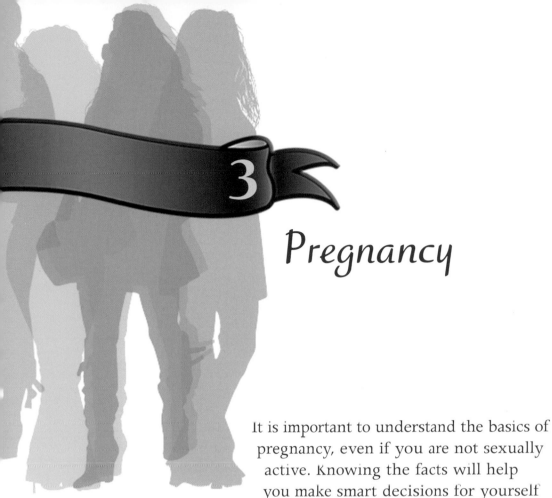

3

Pregnancy

It is important to understand the basics of pregnancy, even if you are not sexually active. Knowing the facts will help you make smart decisions for yourself when the time comes. If you are sexually active, it is even more crucial for you to be aware of what happens to your body during pregnancy.

Fertilization

Fertilization occurs when a male's sperm unites with a female's egg. This moment, called conception, usually happens during vaginal intercourse or shortly after intercourse. In vaginal intercourse, a male's erect penis is inserted into the female's vagina. The friction caused by the movement of the penis in and out of the vagina stimulates the sex organs. When this sexual stimulation reaches

This color-enhanced image shows several sperm attempting to fertilize an egg. The surface of the fallopian tube is seen in the background.

its peak in the male, he has an orgasm and ejaculates. During ejaculation, the male's semen is deposited in the female's vagina. Semen is fluid that contains sperm.

When a male ejaculates inside the female's vagina, sperm travel through the cervix into the female's uterus, then make their way into the fallopian tubes. Sperm are so tiny that you need a microscope to see them. When a man ejaculates, the semen that is released (usually less than 1 teaspoonful) contains millions of sperm. It's a long journey for the tiny sperm, and most die in the process. Typically, just a few thousand sperm successfully reach each fallopian tube. Of those thousand, only one is needed to fertilize the egg and create a pregnancy.

Some sperm can reach the fallopian tubes in just minutes, but others may take hours. Once they are inside the fallopian tubes, sperm can live for forty-eight to seventy-two hours. After a female ovulates, it takes the egg about seventy-two hours to travel through the fallopian tube. If any sperm meet up with an egg making its way down one of the fallopian tubes to the uterus, fertilization may result.

The Egg

The egg is covered with two layers of cells that a sperm must get through in order to fertilize it. Inside the rounded head of the sperm—the acrosome—are chemicals that dig a hole into the egg's protective covering. Many sperm may start to penetrate the egg's layers, but only one can usually get inside. When this sperm makes it inside the egg, the egg lets off chemicals that make it impossible for other sperm to enter.

When the sperm's chromosomes join with the egg's chromosomes, fertilization is complete. Chromosomes are tiny, rod-shaped structures that are found in the nucleus, or center, of both male and female sex cells. Chromosomes contain genes, which are passed down from generation to generation and are responsible for a person's unique traits.

The Embryo

The fertilized egg, which is smaller than a grain of sand, is called a zygote. It normally contains forty-six chromosomes: twenty-three from the egg, and twenty-three from the sperm. Before it reaches the uterus, the zygote undergoes several changes. After fertilization, it moves through the fallopian tube toward the uterus. The zygote begins to divide—one cell becomes two cells, two become four, four become eight, and so on. The zygote is now called an embryo.

In rare cases, the embryo implants outside of the uterus, usually in a fallopian tube. This type of implantation, called an ectopic pregnancy, rarely results in a successful birth. In addition, it can be dangerous and painful for the mother, so it must be discovered and treated.

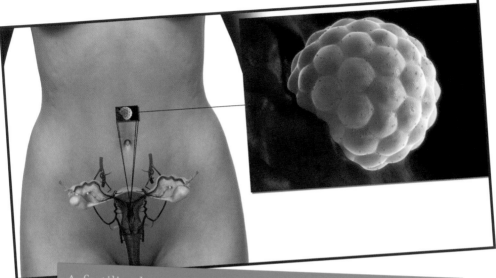

A fertilized egg divides into a ball of cells *(inset)*, which implants itself in the lining of the uterus. This marks the beginning of a pregnancy.

If all goes well, the embryo reaches the uterus about three days after fertilization and implants itself in the uterine lining. The embryo then begins to secrete a hormone called human chorionic gonadotropin (hCG). This hormone stops the menstrual cycle, so the pregnant female no longer gets her period during her pregnancy. When a woman has a positive pregnancy test result, the hormone that causes the positive result is hCG.

If you are sexually active, the following are often signs of pregnancy. If you are experiencing any of these signs individually, it probably doesn't mean you're pregnant. However, if you have several or all of these symptoms, you should consult your doctor:

- A missed or abnormally light period
- Sore, tender breasts
- Increased fatigue
- Increased nausea
- Change in appetite
- More frequent urination

From Embryo to Fetus

Within the first two weeks of pregnancy, structures that will help the embryo grow begin to form in the uterus. One of these

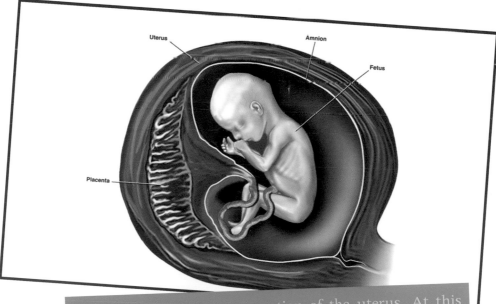

A fetus shown in a cross-section of the uterus. At this stage of development (sixteen to twenty weeks), the fetus is clearly human.

structures is a disk-shaped organ called the placenta. It is attached to the umbilical cord, which connects the mother's uterus to the baby's umbilicus, or navel. In this way, the placenta serves to remove the embryo's waste materials and supply the embryo with oxygen and nutrients from the pregnant woman's body. In addition, the placenta produces hormones that control the embryo's development. Another structure that begins to develop is the amnion, a thin membrane or sac that fills with fluid (amniotic fluid) to surround and protect the embryo as it grows into a fetus.

The embryo's major organs start to form between the third and eighth week of pregnancy. The embryo is about 1 inch (2.5 cm) long and weighs about half an ounce (0.01 kilograms) by the end of the second month. Around the ninth week, the baby's body begins to grow, and its organs begin to develop. From this point until childbirth, the baby is called a fetus. During the first three months of the fetus stage, the length of the fetus increases dramatically, growing as much as 2 inches (5 cm) each month. During the last months of pregnancy, the weight of the fetus greatly increases as well.

Pregnancy usually lasts for roughly nine months. Pregnancy is divided into three equal parts, or trimesters. Each trimester lasts three months. At the end of the third trimester, just before childbirth, an average fetus is about 20 inches (51 cm) long and weighs about 7 pounds (3 kg).

Labor and Birth

Toward the end of the pregnancy, the woman's body floods with hormones that prepare her body for labor and delivery.

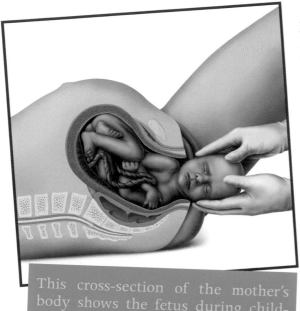
This cross-section of the mother's body shows the fetus during childbirth. Between 93 and 97 percent of babies emerge headfirst.

During labor, the child is pushed out of the uterus. The process of labor is divided into three stages.

During the first stage, a woman experiences labor pains—discomfort caused by muscles in the uterus as they tense up and then relax. Then the cervix softens and dilates, or opens. When the cervix has fully dilated—about 4 inches (10 cm) in diameter—the second stage begins. Muscle contractions in the uterus and abdomen begin to push the baby through the cervix, and then through the vagina.

The third stage begins once the baby is born. It ends when the placenta—the organ that has been nourishing the baby inside the womb—is pushed out of the uterus and vagina.

Infertility

Infertility is the term used to describe a couple's inability to produce children through sexual intercourse. Sometimes, the man has a problem with his reproductive system, which affects the sperm in his semen. Other times, the woman has a blockage of her fallopian tubes, keeping her eggs from reaching the uterus. There are many reasons for infertility.

One of the common causes of infertility in women is pelvic inflammatory disease (PID). This disease can be caused by an improperly treated bacterial sexually transmitted disease (STD), such as chlamydia. Each year in the United States, more than one million women experience an episode of pelvic inflammatory disease. About one in eight women with PID end up infertile.

Damage can be serious if an STD spreads to internal reproductive organs. Vulnerable organs include the cervix, uterus, fallopian tubes, and ovaries. Left untreated, PID can cause permanent damage to these organs by turning healthy tissue into scar tissue. Fortunately, there are methods besides sexual intercourse that can help an infertile couple to bear children.

Artificial Insemination

Artificial insemination is a procedure in which semen is injected into a woman's uterus. Sometimes the male's semen is "washed" to remove unhealthy sperm, antibodies, and seminal fluid that could be rejected by the female's uterus. At the doctor's office, the healthy sperm are placed directly inside the uterus using a fine tube called a catheter. If the male's sperm aren't capable of fertilization, donor sperm may be used.

Laser Surgery

Laser surgery may help cure some kinds of infertility, especially when the cause is a blockage in the fallopian tubes. In this procedure, an intense beam of light is aimed at the blockage to break it apart. Some physicians, however, believe the dangers involved in laser surgery are not worth the risk.

MYTHS & FACTS

MYTH You can't get pregnant during your period.

FACT You can get pregnant during your period. Because a woman's cycle is not 100 percent predictable, and sperm can survive several days after intercourse, there is no guaranteed "safe" time to have sex.

MYTH You can't get pregnant the first time you have sex.

FACT You only have to have unprotected sex once to get pregnant, and it can be the first time.

MYTH If you are not sexually active, there is no need to see a gynecologist.

FACT Traditionally, doctors have advised women to have their first gynecological checkup when they become sexually active or have reached the age of eighteen, whichever comes first. But at any point, you may want to visit a gynecologist to talk about periods, birth control, and sexually transmitted diseases (STDs). There are many reasons why you might need to see a gynecologist. If you are experiencing irregular or unusually heavy periods, if you are worried because you have never gotten your period, or if you think you may have a vaginal infection (which may not be sexually transmitted), it's a good idea to make an appointment, no matter what your age.

MYTHS & FACTS

MYTH If you have a sexually transmitted disease, you would have symptoms.

FACT A woman can have an STD, but not show any symptoms. Regular checkups and protecting yourself are the best ways to stay healthy.

In Vitro Fertilization

In vitro fertilization is a method that enables a woman to get pregnant without intercourse. In this process, eggs are removed from the female's ovary and fertilized by the male's sperm in a dish in a laboratory. (*In vitro* means "in glass.") Microscopic instruments are used in this procedure. During an office visit, the fertilized eggs are implanted directly into the female's uterus. Donor eggs can be used if the female's eggs are damaged.

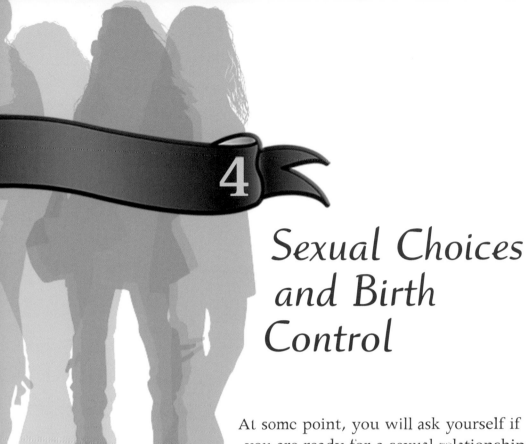

4

Sexual Choices and Birth Control

At some point, you will ask yourself if you are ready for a sexual relationship. This is a very personal issue—no one knows the answer but you. If you don't know for sure if you're ready, then you're not, no matter what anyone else might try to tell you. But if and when you do decide that you're ready, you must know the facts about birth control. Whether or not to get pregnant is one of the biggest decisions you'll ever make in your life, and it should be just that—your decision.

Abstinence

Abstinence is the decision not to have sex. Having unprotected sexual intercourse just one time, even if it's your very first time, can result in pregnancy. So, when it comes to sexual choices,

Many couples choose to abstain from intercourse until after they are married. Giving your virginity to your new spouse creates a special bond.

abstinence is a valid and worthwhile option. It is the only 100 percent effective method of birth control. Sex is a very mature act that can have some serious consequences. Deciding whether to have sex is one of the first important life decisions you will make for yourself.

If you choose abstinence, you are far from alone, even if it sometimes feels as if you are the only one you know who is not sexually active. A recent U.S. government study found that 50 percent of women between the ages of fifteen and nineteen have never had sex. Many people believe that it is best for a girl to lose her virginity to her husband, after getting married. This may seem old-fashioned, but it is a decision that has many positive consequences.

Abstinence from vaginal intercourse is the only sure way to avoid pregnancy. Abstinence also can mean avoiding oral and anal sex, too. If this is your choice, it is a sure-fire way to prevent all STDs. The desire not to contract sexually transmitted diseases is one of the main reasons why many young people today are choosing abstinence.

Birth Control

For girls who decide against abstinence, the choices regarding sex are more complex. Some may think that using birth control products (also called contraceptives) is "too much trouble," or that these products "ruin the mood." The simple fact is that the few moments it takes to use contraceptives can prevent an unintended pregnancy. Condoms and certain other contraceptives also offer some protection against such STDs as herpes, chlamydia, gonorrhea, and human immunodeficiency virus (HIV), the virus that causes acquired immunodeficiency syndrome (AIDS). To prevent conception, contraceptives must be used properly every single time a person has sexual intercourse.

Types of Birth Control

If you are sexually active, or plan on becoming sexually active, make an appointment with a gynecologist. This is a health-care provider who specializes in the female body and reproductive system. The gynecologist will help determine what form of birth control is best for you. You should also talk to your partner, a close friend, a parent, or another trusted adult to help you make a decision. Discussing birth control can be awkward and scary. It means not only talking about sex, but also talking about trust and honesty. If you are not able to talk about these things with your partner, you are probably not ready to be sexually active with him.

Many different kinds of birth control methods are available. If you do not like one method, you can always try another. Ask yourself four things when deciding on the form of birth control that is best for you and your partner:

- How effective is it in preventing pregnancy and diseases?
- How safe is it?
- Will it fit into my lifestyle?
- Can I afford it?

Some birth control methods are more effective and safe than others. If a contraceptive drug or device is not used in the right way, it may not work properly, and you will run the risk of an unintended pregnancy. Use of each type of method requires advance planning. Some kinds of birth control can be put in place hours before sex, while others must be used right before having sex. Only the morning-after pill can be used after sex. Partly due to its potentially serious side effects, the morning-after pill is for emergency use only, not routine contraception.

The Rhythm Method

Using the rhythm method means that a man and woman do not have sex during the time of the month when the woman is ovulating. This isn't a very effective method of birth control because sperm can live inside the vagina for several days. Therefore, a woman who does not want to get pregnant should not have sex for a few days before and five days after she ovulates. However, it can be difficult to predict accurately the exact moment of ovulation. This is especially true for teens, since their menstrual cycles are still regulating themselves. The rhythm method does not protect against STDs.

Withdrawal

When a man uses withdrawal, he takes his penis out of the woman's vagina before he ejaculates. This method is ineffective because semen can leak out of the penis inside the woman's vagina before ejaculation. It also can be difficult for a man to withdraw before he ejaculates because ejaculation and orgasm don't always occur at exactly the same time. Withdrawal does not protect a person from STDs.

Diaphragm

A diaphragm looks like a little rubber bowl. To be used correctly, the diaphragm should be filled with spermicide (a chemical that kills sperm) and inserted into the vagina so that it covers the cervical opening. The diaphragm's job is to stop sperm from getting inside the uterus. If any sperm manage to get around the diaphragm, the spermicide is supposed to kill them. A woman can be fitted by a gynecologist to ensure that the diaphragm is the proper size for her body. The diaphragm is an effective method of birth control when used properly. However, it does not protect against STDs.

Condoms have a high failure rate if they are used incorrectly. Old condoms and those that have been improperly stored are liable to leak or break.

Condoms

A condom is a very thin sheath of rubber that fits over a male's erect penis. It is put on before sexual intercourse takes place and acts as a barrier between sexual partners, and in the case of vaginal intercourse, between a male's sperm and a female's egg. Because a condom prevents the exchange of fluids, it's rather effective in protecting against pregnancy and STDs.

Reality Female Condoms

The female condom resembles the male condom, except that it is larger and has a ring on the inside. The woman squeezes the inner ring and inserts it into her vagina until it hits the cervix. The outer rim covers the labia (lips of the vagina) and the penis during sexual intercourse. Used properly, the female condom is between 79 and 95 percent effective at preventing pregnancy.

Spermicides

Spermicides are chemicals that kill sperm. They come as vaginal suppositories, film, foam, gels, and creams. They are designed to be used with condoms, diaphragms, and cervical caps in order to make these forms of birth control more effective. Used alone, spermicides range from being less than 50 percent to 94 percent effective in preventing pregnancy. Spermicides do not protect against sexually transmitted diseases.

The Pill

The Pill is a reliable method of birth control, and it can be easy to use. A woman takes one Pill each day, in a twenty-eight-day cycle. The Pill contains synthetic (manufactured) hormones similar to the estrogen and progesterone produced by a woman's ovaries when she is pregnant. The presence of these synthetic hormones makes the body think there's a pregnancy, so the ovaries don't release any new eggs.

As each contraceptive pill is labeled with a day of the week, it is easy for a woman to tell if she has missed a day.

The Pill can be prescribed by a gynecologist and comes in convenient packages that contain a twenty-eight-day supply. Usually, when on the cycle, a woman takes real hormone pills for twenty-one days, and then she takes a sugar pill for seven days, which causes her to resume her menstrual cycle. The pills must be taken every day at the same time to be most effective.

A newer kind of oral contraceptive pill changes a woman's menstrual cycle so that she has only four periods per year. This drug is taken for eighty-four consecutive days before taking a break to resume menstruation.

Other, even newer contraceptive drugs are designed to effectively put an end to a woman's menstrual cycle for a year. In addition, these drugs thin out the uterine lining, making it even less likely that a fertilized egg will become embedded to begin a pregnancy. Researchers say these new drugs are safe, but long-term studies have yet to be completed. When used alone, none of the pills mentioned above protects against STDs.

Depo-Provera

Depo-Provera is another synthetic hormone that can be used as a contraceptive. Similar to the Pill, Depo-Provera tricks the body into thinking that it is pregnant, so a woman's ovaries stop releasing ova. The difference is that Depo-Provera is injected into the woman once every eleven weeks, rather than being taken more often in pill form. Depo-Provera has side effects similar to the Pill. It can cause weight gain, increased breast size, headaches, or depression. This form of birth control does not protect against STDs.

In Conclusion

As this book tries to point out, the female reproductive system is a wonder of nature. So much is known about the reproductive process, but a lot is still mysterious. When you become capable of reproducing, the changes in girls' bodies and attitudes bring up numerous questions and issues. You might ask yourself: How and why does my body produce eggs? Why do I feel irritable before I get my period? Am I ready to have sex? Am I ready to have a baby? How is it possible that a baby can grow inside me? What is the best way for me to avoid getting pregnant?

Perhaps after reading this book, you now have a better idea of the body parts and bodily functions that allow you to reproduce. Ultimately, the more you know about yourself, the better decision you'll be able to make when it comes to staying happy and healthy.

Glossary

acrosome Structure found in the head of sperm that contains chemicals that eat through an egg's protective layers.

Bartholin's glands Small glands found on both sides of the vaginal opening that secrete fluid.

cervix Narrow part of the uterus that is connected to the vagina.

chromosome Rod-like structure in the nucleus of a cell that contains hereditary information.

clitoris Small, sensitive organ found at the top of the vestibule in females; its primary function is to produce pleasure.

contraceptive Drug or device used to prevent pregnancy.

ejaculation Sudden release of semen through the penis.

embryo Unborn child in the first eight weeks of development.

estrogen Hormone that is responsible for the development of female sexual characteristics.

fallopian tube Slender organ that carries an egg from the ovary to the uterus. It also carries the sperm from the uterus toward the ovary.

fertilization Joining of the male sperm and the female egg.

fetus Unborn child from about the eighth week of development until childbirth.

gamete Mature female or male sex cell; the egg or the sperm.

gynecologist Health-care provider who specializes in the female body and reproductive system.

human chorionic gonadotropin (hCG) Hormone produced by the embryo and fetus.

hymen Thin piece of skin that covers the vaginal opening.

hypothalamus Part of the brain that secretes hormones that regulate various body processes.

labia majora Outer lips of the vagina.

labia minora Inner lips of the vagina.

menstruation Monthly discharge of blood from the lining of the uterus.

mons veneris Fatty, hair-covered pad of tissue that covers the female's pubic bone.

orgasm Series of pleasurable muscle contractions that occur at the peak of sexual excitement.

ovary One of a pair of female sex glands in which hormones and female sex cells, or ova, are produced.

ovulation The release of an egg by the ovary.

pituitary gland Gland at the base of the brain that secretes hormones that regulate many body processes.

placenta Organ that connects a fetus to the mother's uterus. It provides the fetus with oxygen and food and removes fetal waste.

progesterone Female hormone secreted by the ovaries.

semen Sticky, greyish-white fluid that is expelled from the penis during ejaculation. It contains sperm.

sexually transmitted disease (STD) A disease spread through sexual intercourse.

urethra Duct through which urine leaves the body.

uterus Female organ in which an unborn child is contained and nourished until birth. Also called the womb.

vagina The opening to a woman's inner reproductive organs.

vestibule Area between the labia minora.

vulva A woman's outer genital area.

zygote Fertilized egg.

For More Information

CDC National STD Hotline
(800) 227-8922
En Español: (800) 344-7432 (Monday–Friday, 8am–2am EST)

Center for Young Women's Health
Children's Hospital Boston
333 Longwood Avenue, 5th Floor
Boston, MA 02115
(617) 355-2994
Web site: http://www.youngwomenshealth.org

Centers for Disease Control and Prevention
1600 Clifton Road
Atlanta, GA 30333
(404) 639-3534
Web site: http://www.cdc.gov/nchstp/dstd/disease_info.htm

National Women's Health Information Center
Office on Women's Health
U.S. Department of Health and Human Services
8270 Willow Oaks Corporate Drive, Suite 301
Fairfax, VA 22031
Web site: http://www.girlshealth.gov

Office on Women's Health
U.S. Department of Health and Human Services
200 Independence Avenue SW, Room 712E
Washington, DC 20201
(202) 690-7650
Web site: www.4woman.gov

Planned Parenthood Federation of America
National Headquarters
434 West 33rd Street
New York, NY 10001
(212) 541-7800
Web site: http://www.plannedparenthood.org

Web Sites

Due to the changing nature of Internet links, Rosen Publishing has developed an online list of Web sites related to the subject of this book. This site is updated regularly. Please use this link to access the list:

http://www.rosenlinks.com/gh/fere

For Further Reading

Boston Women's Health Book Collective. *Our Bodies, Ourselves: A New Edition for a New Era.* New York, NY: Touchstone, 2005.

Harris, Robie H. *It's Perfectly Normal: Changing Bodies, Growing Up, Sex, and Sexual Health.* Cambridge, MA: Candlewick Press, 2004.

Loulan, Joann, and Bonnie Worthen. *Period. A Girl's Guide to Menstruation.* Minnetonka, MN: Book Peddlers, 2001.

Madaras, Lynda. *The "What's Happening to My Body?" Book for Girls: A Growing-Up Guide for Parents and Daughters.* New York, NY: Newmarket Press, 2000.

Stanley, Deborah. *Sexual Health Information for Teens: Health Tips About Sexual Development, Human Reproduction, and Sexually Transmitted Diseases* (Teen Health Series). Detroit, MI: Omnigraphics, 2003.

Bibliography

Boston Women's Health Book Collective. *Our Bodies, Ourselves: A New Edition for a New Era*. New York, NY: Touchstone, 2005.

Britannica Online. "Human Reproductive System." Retrieved August 2006 (http://www.search.eb.com/eb/article-9110811).

Manassiev, Nikolai, and Malcolm I. Whitehead, eds. *Female Reproductive Health*. Abingdon, UK: Taylor & Francis, 2003.

McCloskey, Jenny. *Your Sexual Health*. San Francisco, CA: Halo Books, 1993.

WebMD. "Sexual Health: Your Guide to the Female Reproductive System." Retrieved August 2006 (http://www.webmd.com/content/article/9/2953_484.htm).

WebMD. "Sexual Health: Your Guide to Premenstrual Syndrome." Retrieved August 2006 (http://www.webmd.com/content/article/10/2953_497.htm).

Index

Photo Credits

Cover, pp. 1, 3, 4, 5, 19 © www.istockphoto.com; pp. 7, 15, 17, 26 © Articulate Graphics/Custom Medical Stock Photo; p. 10 © Marwan Naamani/AFP/Getty Images; p. 11 © www.istockphoto.com/Deanna Quinton; p. 13 © Visuals Unlimited/Corbis; pp. 20, 25 Illustration Copyright © 2007 Nucleus Medical Art, All rights reserved. www.nucleusinc.com; p. 22 © Yorgos Nikas/Stone/ Getty Images; p. 24 © 3D4Medical/Getty Images; p. 32 © www.istockphoto. com/Gunther Beck; p. 36 © www.istockphoto.com/Dan Brandenburg; p. 38 © www.istockphoto.com/EauClaire Media.

Designer: Evelyn Horovicz; **Editor:** Christopher Roberts
Photo Researcher: Amy Feinberg